The Guide to
Shakespearean London Theatres

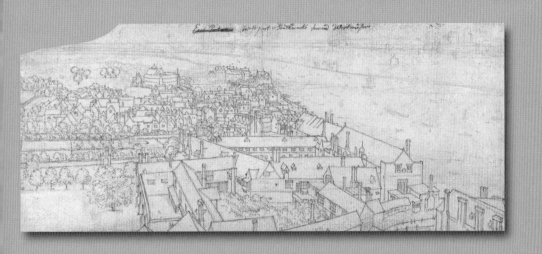

The Guide to
SHAKESPEAREAN
LONDON THEATRES

PETER SILLITOE

EDITED BY MAURICE HINDLE

SHaLT

CONTENTS

Preface

LONDON'S FIRST COMMERCIAL THEATRES appeared north and south of the city before Shakespeare was a teenager. At first they were occupied by touring companies who ranged over the whole country, making brief stopovers in London. But within a decade of the first theatres in 1575, great new plays began to appear, with the result that the touring companies started to find it more profitable to stay in the one place to exhibit their new delights. Fresh playwrights arrived. Thomas Kyd's one great play from the 1580s survives, although he died at the age of only thirty-six, after being tortured by government agents. Six of Christopher Marlowe's survive, although he died in 1593 at only twenty-nine, killed by government spies. Shakespeare survived well beyond these first writers, producing nearly forty plays in all. His younger friend Ben Jonson lived even longer, writing plays and verse throughout his long career. All these and many more produced plays which in effect created the English drama that has survived down to the present day.

We now know something of the remains and sites for more than fifteen of the early theatres built for Shakespeare and his fellows between 1575 and 1629. ShaLT's aim is chiefly to locate all these sites, whether they survive from archaeological digs or only exist as markings on early maps. We have indicated their locations on a map of modern London, so that a simple walk around the streets of the city and its immediate environs can identify where they were, and sometimes what remains of them. The first theatres were built in the city's suburbs, but four city inns were used in the early days. Then, probably in 1594, the Lord Mayor persuaded the Privy Council to ban the use of these inns as theatres. After that, the number of playhouses grew, at first around the city of London's perimeter, where the Lord Mayor had no control, but also in the precincts of Saint Paul's and the Blackfriars inside the city, where the mayor's rule did not run.

This Guide and its map tell the story of the companies of professional actors who performed in London's playhouses between 1575 and 1642, when the development of civil war closed all the theatres. That catastrophic event kept plays out of London for eighteen years, and the new theatres that opened with the Restoration of King Charles II had wholly different ideas of performance, and wholly different theatres. This tells the story of the Shakespearean theatres preceding that long closure.

ANDREW GURR

1. A miniature of Henry Wriothesley, the third Earl of Southampton (1594), to whom Shakespeare dedicated his two narrative poems, *Venus and Adonis* (1593) and *The Rape of Lucrece* (1594). In the same month as *The Rape of Lucrece* was published Shakespeare joined the Chamberlain's Men playing company.

Introduction

IN 1576, IN THE MIDDLE of the reign of Elizabeth I, actor and entrepreneur James Burbage opened the 'Theatre' in the east London suburb of Shoreditch, just under two miles north east of St Paul's cathedral [Map Legend reference: ML12]. This was the first time a purpose-built theatre had opened its doors in the British Isles since Roman times a thousand years earlier. Burbage's Theatre was an immediate success. For the next sixty years new playhouses emerged as a Tudor and Stuart theatre-land was born. This new theatre industry made Burbage famous, giving work to Christopher Marlowe, William Shakespeare, Ben Jonson, and many others. Playhouse owners and actors quickly realized the stage could delight large audiences with fights, speeches, hilarious comedies, or violent stories of revenge.

For many people today 'Shakespearean theatre' suggests the dramatic output of only one man, William Shakespeare, and his Globe. Knowledge of such theatre nowadays frequently ends there, apart from a couple of other playwrights. Yet 'Shakespearean theatre' encompasses the entire period of London playhouses, plays and players, from the 1570s right through to the English civil wars that made Parliament close down the entire theatre industry in 1642.

'Shakespearean theatre' along with Shakespeare's life and work, refers to the careers of many other writers, actors, playgoers, and playhouse entrepreneurs in this period. Although modern theatregoers may know other playwrights such as Marlowe, Jonson, and perhaps John Webster and Thomas Middleton, this seventy-year period witnessed a massive body of dramatic work written by dozens of writers, an estimated 3000 plays, 600 of which survive. This epoch of dramatic ingenuity created a huge theatrical industry. Without it, British theatre as we know it could not have developed.

Hæc est regia illa totius Angliæ ciuitas LONDINVM unam Thamesim sita. Cæsari, ut plures exis sinuit. Tri nuncupata. multarum gentium commercio nobilitata, ædibus don plis, excelsa arcibus, claris vigeniis, viris omnium artium doctrin re præstantibus, percelebri. Deniq; omnium rerum copia, atque op mirabilis. Iacuit in eam totius orbi opes ipsi Thamasis, mercarijs sescensia millia passuum, ad urbem præaltis aluec nauegabilis.

2. An engraving made and coloured in 1572, showing London before the first playhouses were built to the north and south of the City.

LONDINVM FERACISSIMI AN-
GLIAE REGNI METROPOLIS.

The Spent fielde

THE TOWRE

STILLIARDS) Hanfa, Gothica dicto, conuentum, vel congregationem fonans, mul-
turum ciuitatum eft confoederata Societas, tum ob praefixa Regibus, ac Ducib. benefi-
cia : tum ob fecuram terra, marique, mercatura tractationem, tum denique, ad tran-
quillam Rerumpub. pacem, & ad modeftam adolefcentum inftitutionem conferuan-
dam, inftituta: plurimoru Regum ac Principum, maxime Angliae, Galliae, Daniae, ac
Magnae Mifcouiae, nec non Flandriae, ac Brabantiae Du cum priuilegiis, ac immuni-
tatib. exornatu fuit. Habet ea quatuor Emporia, (vntores quidam vocant, in quibus
ciuitatum negotiatores refident, fuaque mercatus exercent.Hor. alterum fci. Lond-
ni, domeftica oeconomia nitet, habens domum Gildehalld Teutonica,qua vulgo Stilliard, nuncupat

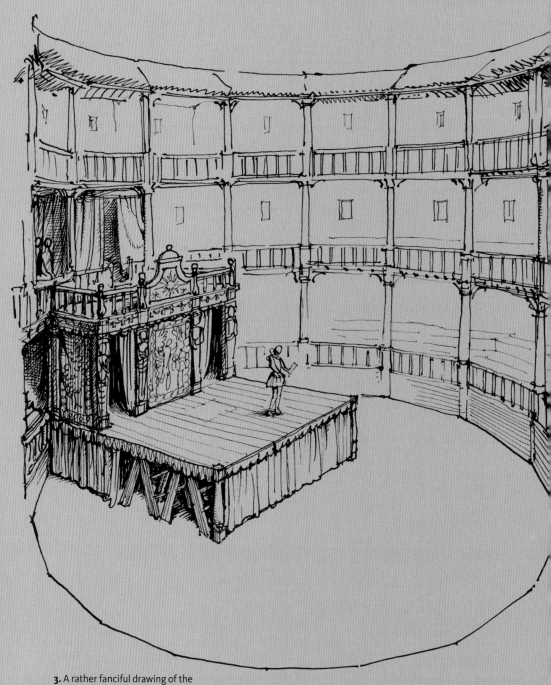

3. A rather fanciful drawing of the interior of an Elizabethan playhouse by C. Walter Hodges which he dates 'c.1576', suggesting he had The Theatre in mind when producing it.

The Elizabethan stage:
the birth of London theatre

From Scaffold to Hall: What is an Elizabethan Playhouse?

T HE VERY EARLIEST USE of a space for putting on plays in return for a spectator's entrance fee in the Elizabethan period came in 1567, when the Red Lion theatre opened near Mile End [ML11]. Yet the Red Lion cannot be counted as the first playhouse, since it appears to have been a very basic and short-lived scaffold-stage rather than a purpose-built playhouse. Indeed, during our period, theatres developed in striking forms. They changed from occupying outside spaces through the open-air theatres with galleries, like James Burbage's 1576 Theatre and the later well-known Rose and Globe playhouses [ML11, 18, 20], to using indoor hall playhouses, design-shifts that started the 'theatre-land' of today's west end.

Burbage's Theatre

A large timber polygonal building built to house audiences of thousands in its yard and three tiers of gallery space, the Theatre provided the model for all the amphitheatre-style houses that followed. Its historical importance cannot be overstressed. It was where Shakespeare's early plays were staged. Financially it was a great success. Excavated by an archeological team from the Museum of London in 2008–10, its polygonal shape suggests that Burbage wanted to make the Roman design a prominent feature, persuading Londoners that they were now living in a new kind of Rome, or Troy.

The first Elizabethan theatres were aimed at all levels of society. Almost three thousand spectators crammed together in the larger outdoor playhouses, a thousand of them paying a penny to listen and watch as 'groundlings'. Those with more money could pay to sit in the galleries in comfort, with a roof and an elevated view of the stage. Beer and snacks such as nuts were sold to the spectators.

4. Portrait of Queen Elizabeth I from a miniature.

The Four Inns

Theatre historians have only recently realized the importance of the city inns for playing. Two provided outdoor yards, the other two rooms to play indoors. Located within the City limits, the inns offered performance spaces for the early acting companies. The Bel Savage off Ludgate Hill near St Paul's [ML5] was used by Elizabeth's own players, the Queen's Men, with its famed extempore clown Richard Tarlton. The Bull in Bishopsgate Street [ML3] hosted playing as early as 1575, like the Bell at Bell Inn Yard [ML4]. The Cross Keys [ML6] was certainly staging plays by 1579.

Elizabethan Indoor Theatre and the Boy Actors

From early on 'boy companies' also performed plays, but indoors. They used a playhouse in the Almoner's hall of the old cathedral [ML1], while another indoor theatre staged plays at Blackfriars. They regularly performed before Queen Elizabeth and her court having been trained in acting and singing (Paul's boys were choristers). In 1582 Stephen Gosson remarked that 'Cupid and Psyche [were] played at Paul's and a great many comedies more at the Blackfriars and in every playhouse in London.'

5. Actor Richard Tarlton playing pipe and drum.

The boy actors of St Paul's and the Blackfriars competed with the adult companies of Burbage's Theatre, since both staged plays for paying audiences. On the other hand, the indoor boy companies were putting on a rather different kind of drama. In the 1570s there is nothing to suggest that the boy actors shared plays with the outdoor Theatre or Curtain, or the smaller playing spaces of the four inns. The new theatrical industry branched out in many directions, targeting different social orders.

Rising Demand: the Queen's Men and Court Revels

By 1580 a number of the new playhouses had been operating for several years, with the Theatre and the Curtain in the northern suburbs, together with the four City inns and the two boys' companies at St Paul's and Blackfriars, and the only theatre south of the river at Newington Butts. One reason for the growth of the theatrical industry must have been its capacity to engage and entertain the ever-expanding population of London. In 1580 around 100,000 people lived there, but by about 1600 this had doubled to 200,000, and we must imagine a related rise in the playgoing habit. The playing companies continued to tour the

6. The yard of a City inn, with a booth stage erected for staging plays, as imagined by C. Walter Hodges.

country playing in great houses, but also at the playhouses in
Shoreditch, besides the four inns of the City of London. Ordinary
men and women could enjoy a play while taking their drink,
much in the way as courtiers and the wealthy did.

   In 1583 the Queen decided it was time that a new company
should be formed, and gave it her own name, the Queen's Men.
She wished to create the 'best' company, and gave it a monopoly
on performances at court for the next five years. Since the
Queen's Men sported such a prestigious title, their tours of the

country and performances at the new London theatres brought them twice what other companies could command.

Performances by the Queen's Men obviously provided the most privileged type of playing, but others still attracted great numbers. This is clear from the publication during the early 1580s of anti-theatrical tracts. In one attack, the writer argued that 'theatres and unclean assemblies' were home 'to idleness, unthriftiness, whoredom, wantonness, drunkenness, and what not'. But soon the status of actors was not to be scorned. The Mayor of London had to allow the Queen's Men to perform at the four City inns in an official capacity. London playing was becoming more centralized both in terms of court influence and in terms of its location in the City's urban spaces.

Henslowe's Rose and Bankside Theatre

Without an audience paying to see plays they liked, nobody in the business could turn a profit. Companies not only competed with each other, but also with the bear and bull-baiting arenas. Many of the playhouses could be found in areas associated with prostitution, and there is ample evidence that prostitutes frequented the new playhouses. The large crowds that plays attracted were good for all kinds of business.

By the late 1580s both the Theatre and the Curtain [ML13] had been operating successfully for well over ten years, the four inns and Newington Butts [ML17] were still active, and four adult companies operated in parallel to the boy actors of Paul's and Blackfriars. In 1587 a third outdoor theatre was built, the Rose [ML18] on Bankside. More is known about the Rose than any other London playhouse because of the dig revealing its foundations carried out in 1989. The Rose was easily accessible on foot across London's (only) bridge, or by wherry.

Playgoing Comes of Age:
Thomas Kyd's *The Spanish Tragedy*

After about 1587 or 1588 (the year of the Spanish Armada) there was a sudden improvement in the quality and therefore impact of new plays. Two key playwrights became notable, pre-dating Shakespeare's appearance by four or five years: Kyd and Marlowe. Kyd's revenge play *The Spanish Tragedy* became the most popular play of the entire Shakespearean period, performed on and off for nearly sixty years, and going through numerous printed editions. There is some agreement that the play's anti-Spanish content (it is set in a corrupt Catholic court in Spain) suggests it was written to appeal to an audience familiar with the failed 1588 invasion of England by Spain's huge Armada of ships. The play was the first Elizabethan theatrical blockbuster.

7. A cutaway illustration, showing what the Rose playhouse on Bankside might have looked like in its original form before 1592.

The Spanish Tragedy:

Or,

HIERONIMO is mad againe.

Containing the lamentable end of *Don Horatio*,
and *Belimperia*; With the pitifull Death
of HIERONIMO.

Newly Corrected, Amended, and Enlarged with new
Additions, as it hath of late beene divers
times Acted.

LONDON
Printed by *Augustine Mathewes*, for *Francis Grove*, and are to
bee sold at his Shoppe, neere the Sarazens Head,
upon Snow-hill. 1633.

8. The title page of Thomas Kyd's *The Spanish Tragedy*. First staged at about the time of the Spanish Armada in 1588, it remained famous and was regularly staged for the next sixty years.

Christopher Marlowe's two *Tamburlaine* plays and *Dr. Faustus* were amongst the most popular plays of the 1580s. What makes Marlowe significant for us today is the high verbal quality of his writing. Although he usually worked in the tragedy genre Marlowe also produced one play that looked back to the history of the English monarchy, *Edward II*, a work of 'chronicle history'. This was a genre soon to become dominated by Shakespeare following Marlowe's death in 1593.

Early Shakespeare

At some point in the late 1580s (or more likely the very early 1590s) an aspiring actor and dramatist from Warwickshire named William Shakespeare arrived in London and quickly began to author and act in his own plays. Early dramas include his revenge play *Titus Andronicus*, a bloodthirsty tale designed to repeat the gore and sensationalism of *The Spanish Tragedy* in a darkly witty manner, but also his extremely successful early history plays like the three parts of *Henry VI*, and *Richard III*. Beyond these, successful comedies such as *The Taming of the Shrew*, *The Two Gentlemen of Verona* and *The Merchant of Venice* show that, as with the earlier Marlowe, Shakespeare could not only make a name for himself in a short time, but also demonstrate a writing talent that extended into comedic and tragi-comic dramatic genres.

1594: A New Start

When after a long closure for plague the playhouses were reopened in 1594 the Privy Council decided to license two new playing companies: the Chamberlain's Men under their patron the Lord Chamberlain Henry Carey, and the Admiral's Men under their patron Admiral Lord Howard, who had led England to victory against the Spanish Armada. The Chamberlain's were licensed to perform at Burbage's Shoreditch Theatre north of the river in Middlesex, with Shakespeare as resident play-

9. A portrait, thought by some to be of Christopher Marlowe, discovered thirty years ago behind a fireplace in Corpus Christi College Cambridge, where Marlowe was a student.

10. The title page of ChristopherMarlowe's *Tamburlaine*, first printed with its sequel in 1590.

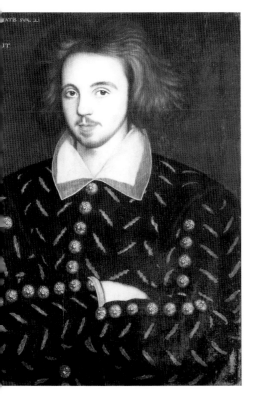

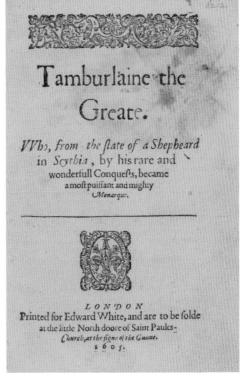

wright, while the Admiral's Men were licensed to play at Henslowe's Rose on Bankside, south of the river in Surrey, with Marlowe's plays predominating. These were now the only two companies licensed to perform in London. This gave the growing masses of playgoers a consistent range of theatre performances to attend every afternoon around 2 pm (all London performances were done in daylight).

Playing at the city's inns was now banned. So in November 1594 Francis Langley started building the Swan playhouse on Bankside [ML19] about 300 yards west of the Rose. To the east the Boar's Head [ML14], a former inn, also soon opened as a playhouse. The boy companies of the 1570s and the four playing inns had all disappeared by 1590, but London now had the Theatre, the Curtain, the Rose, the Swan and the Boar's Head. The theatrical industry of Elizabethan London was thriving.

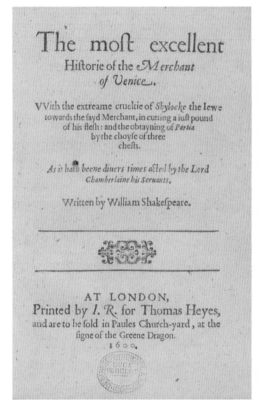

> The moſt excellent
> Hiſtorie of the *Merchant of Venice*.
>
> VVith the extreame cruelie of *Shylocke* the Iewe towards the ſayd Merchant, in cutting a iuſt pound of his fleſh : and the obtayning of *Portia* by the choyſe of three cheſts.
>
> As it hath beene diuers times acted by the Lord Chamberlaine his Seruants.
>
> Written by William Shakeſpeare.
>
> AT LONDON,
> Printed by *I. R.* for Thomas Heyes, and are to be ſold in Paules Church-yard , at the ſigne of the Greene Dragon.
> 1600.

The Bankside Globe

The Globe on Bankside opened in 1599. It stayed in use right up to the 1642 theatre closures. Begun with the timbers of the old Theatre, it was probably made bigger. But the new company of 1594 did not want just an outdoor venue. For winter, they preferred to act indoors, and the inns were now closed to them. So in 1596 James Burbage purchased a £600 freehold on upper-floor rooms at Blackfriars, and built a new indoor theatre for them.

11. Title page for *The Merchant of Venice*, first published in quarto in 1600. The description of its story probably resembles the playbills posted to advertise it.

The vision of the Blackfriars was physically and conceptually brilliantly innovative for adult players. Yet it proved a tricky vision to realise. It could only hold a third of the Theatre's audience, and they had to pay much more for their seats. The well-to-do residents of the Blackfriars precinct strongly objected to a new adult playhouse in their midst. They successfully petitioned the Privy Council to cancel the arrangement. The Burbages were left with a brand new indoor playhouse that could not be used.

Unable to re-negotiate the Theatre lease, for most of 1597 and all of 1598 the Burbage sons were forced to rent the nearby Curtain for their company's performances. In December 1598,

12. Detail from Wenceslas Hollar's 'Long View' of London from the tower of St Mary Overie church (1647). The roof coloured red is the stage cover of the second Globe, built on the foundations of the first Globe.

having lost the use of both Theatre and Blackfriars playhouses, they got the Theatre timbers dismantled and transported across the river, where the Globe was constructed barely 50 yards from Henslowe's Rose. It was built bigger than the Theatre or Rose, and enjoyed a uniquely egalitarian financing and management. Both Burbage brothers plus five other company sharers (including Shakespeare) financed the building and running of the new theatre. From 1599 to 1642 almost all of Shakespeare's plays were performed at the Globe, a fact that in modern times was to help ensure its fame.

The Fortune
In 1600, with the new Globe threatening the livelihood of the smaller Rose, the latter's owners left Southwark and built a new outdoor playhouse, the Fortune, north of the river close to Whitecross Street, a mediaeval market street near today's Barbican arts centre [ML15]. The Chamberlain's Men now dominated Surrey's Bankside suburbs, the Admiral's Men with its Marlowe plays dominating the northern suburbs of Middlesex.

Beyond the Duopoly

Yet this 'duopoly' was ending. Along with the emergence of the Swan and the short-lived Boar's Head, another outdoor playhouse, the Red Bull, [ML16], opened in 1604. As with the Globe and Fortune, the Red Bull in Clerkenwell proved to be of lasting appeal. Like the Globe and the Fortune, it survived until the civil wars, but functioned as a performance space as late as 1661.

Despite the plethora of new playing companies and playhouses in London, it is clear that the 1594 duopoly had allowed the Admiral's Men and Chamberlain's Men to dominate London theatre for a considerable length of time, with all court performances during the period up to 1600 being given by these two competing groups of actors. However, with the Chamberlain's now dominating at the Globe on Surrey's Bankside, and the Admiral's at the immediately popular new Fortune in Middlesex, the 1594 principle of two formally sanctioned playhouses, one north and one south of the river, was restored. In 1600 the Privy Council officially licensed only two playhouses: the Fortune and the Globe.

Beyond Marlowe and Shakespeare: Continued Innovation

New plays were constantly commissioned. The Rose staged dozens of new plays (many now unfortunately lost), including in 1595 an anonymous earlier version of *Henry V* (now lost), Thomas Dekker's *Old Fortunatus*, and in 1599 his popular *The Shoemaker's Holiday*. After 1600, these plays transferred to the Fortune in the north. Although Shakespeare was the dominant writer for the Chamberlain's Men, we must not think that the Burbage company limited themselves to his plays. Satisfying the demands of an audience wanting a constant flow of fresh dramas, they commissioned plays by up-and-coming theatrical writers like Ben Jonson, whose *Every Man in His Humour* featured the acting talents of a certain 'Will. Shakespeare'. In 1597 John Chamberlain wrote about this play: 'we have here a new play of humours in very great request, and I was drawn along to by the common applause, but my opinion of it is (as the fellow said of the shearing of hogs) that there was great cry for so little wool.'

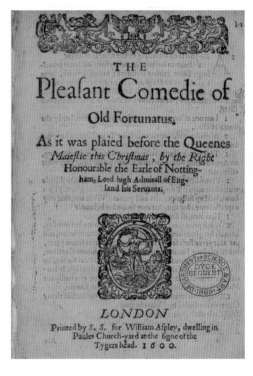

13. The title page of Thomas Dekker's *Old Fortunatus*, revived to celebrate the opening of the Fortune playhouse.

14. Portrait of Benjamin Jonson, poet and playwright, by Abraham van Blyenberch, *c.*1617.

The Last Years of Elizabethan Theatre

Plays were performed to audiences of a comprehensive social mix, from low-paid apprentices to rich aristocrats and courtiers. Audiences were as diverse as their dramatists, a mixed bunch in class and status. The two universities provided the London stage with many playwrights in the period, including Christopher Marlowe and Robert Greene from Cambridge, and John Lyly and George Peele from Oxford. At the same time, Shakespeare and Jonson, perhaps the most famous and successful of all the writers in this age, advanced to the top of their profession in the world of letters and drama without having a university education, coming from humble backgrounds. Studious Ben Jonson succeeded as a poet and playwright despite being the son of a bricklayer, Shakespeare the son of a glover.

The Elizabethan period gave birth to the bombastic tragedies of Kyd and Marlowe, the sophisticated comedies of Lyly for the boy actors, and the comedies and histories of Shakespeare and others. But genre was never fixed or certain, and easily mixed together. Shakespeare's *Richard III* was printed as a tragedy, yet it became classified as a history play in the great Folio of 1623. Similarly, we should remember that the English stage was all-male. Shakespearean theatre only ever featured male actors, the female roles being played by young boys. It was a cross-dressing or transvestite stage, unique to England when compared to continental dramatic practices. It still survives residually to this day in the form of seasonal pantomimes and the like. Young boys learned their trade from the experienced adult actors, sometimes progressing to adult lead roles later in life, whether as a Marlovian tragic hero, or a Shakespearean villain or lover.

15. The Shakespeare bust, in Stratford-upon-Avon.

Court Patronage and City Scorn

In 1603 Elizabeth I died, and her passing marked the end of the Tudors. Before we turn to the time of her successor King James I (James VI of Scotland) we should recall a different side of the story. Not everyone enjoyed or applauded the spectacular rise of theatre.

Any artistic or cultural movement, when it becomes popular, suffers from negative comment. We can trace the emergence of 'anti-theatricalism' when hostility to the theatre began to appear in print. It was heard loudly from the church pulpits. John Northbrooke's *A Treatise Against Dicing, Dancing, Plays and Interludes* (1577), printed only a year after Burbage's Theatre opened, attacked the very notion of players performing to the public. Political authorities in early modern London never spoke with one voice. We must avoid sweeping generalizations, but we can roughly divide society's 'Authorities' into two camps. The Privy Council was the elite body which sought to carry out the will of the Sovereign and Court in legislative matters, while The City wielded its regulatory powers through the decision-making Lord Mayor and his appointed justices. It is fair to see the Privy Council as relatively pro-theatre, since its members such as the Earl of Leicester and the Lord Admiral were patrons of their own theatre companies. On the other hand, the City authorities and the Mayor often sought to close the theatres altogether, citing problems of crowd-control and disruption. There was some potential for trouble when large groups of men and women were allowed to mingle and meet together in public. We know of riots that took place outside the Curtain in the 1580s and 1590s. Epidemics of plague, when the authorities needed to halt the spread of the disease among crowds, meant closing the theatres. Since they could house up to three thousand spectators, this was a sensible health management tactic.

Many citizens of London were Puritans, opposed to the sensuality in plays. Catholics were keener on play-going, since their anti-Puritan energies fed into the theatrical culture of display. When the world of theatre emerged out of the Reformation, anti-Puritan vigour helped to power the popularity of playing and the new theatre industry. Some of the energy that went into Catholic ritual and ceremony was diverted to the playhouse in the form of jigs and dances. Such views on ceremony and display meant that the theatres were disliked by the more puritanical members of the community, who saw such public displays and performances as lewd and deceitful. The pretence intrinsic to theatrical performance therefore became a target for Puritans equally hostile to what they considered idolatrous 'high' church practices of both Anglicans and Catholics.

There were two different types of hostility towards theatres: one concerned with a threat to religious morality, the other concerned with public order and the spread of infectious disease. Such hostility should alert us to a central and positive aspect of the new Shakespearean theatres: these playhouses were for, and accessible to, anyone who could afford to pay a penny for a standing view of the play. The fact that the low-paid working class citizens and apprentices of the capital *did* in great numbers attend the theatres in Elizabethan London should give pause to those who in the twenty-first century associate Shakespeare and other playwrights only with 'high' art and culture.

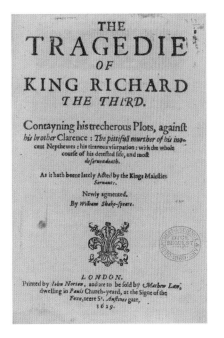

16. The title page of *Richard III* which clearly demonstates it was considered a Tragedy.

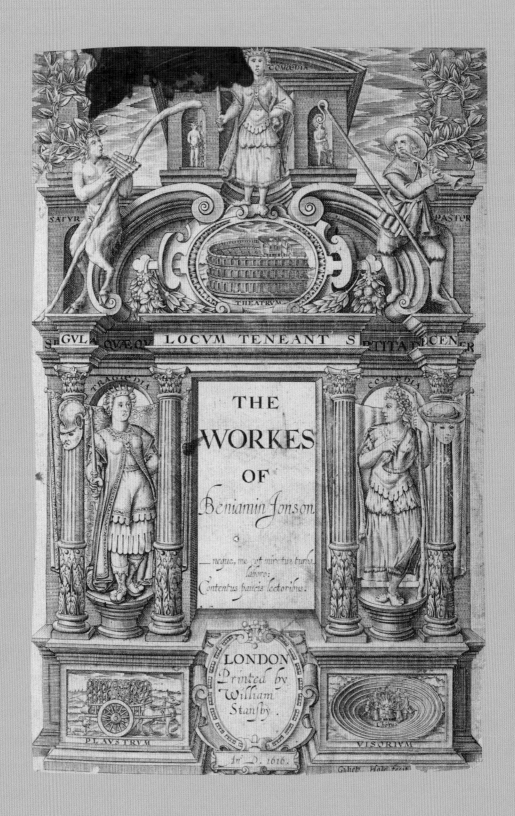

SATYRVS   PASTOR

THEATRVM

SINGVLA QVÆQVE LOCVM TENEANT SORTITA DECENTER

TRAGŒDIA   COMŒDIA

THE
WORKES
OF
Beniamin Jonson

— neque, me ut miretur turba, laboro:
Contentus paucis lectoribus.

LONDON
Printed by
William
Stansby.

PLAVSTRVM   Chorus   VISORIVM

An. D. 1616.

Gulielm. Hole fecit.

The Jacobean Stage:
Royal Patronage

IN 1603, ONE OF KING JAMES'S first actions upon becoming king of England was to make himself patron of the nation's premier playing company, the Chamberlain's Men. Henceforth known as the King's Men, they would wear his scarlet livery when performing special offices for him, as well as being the first choice for the performance of a play at court. The Burbage brothers, Shakespeare and the company sharers now held an unassailable status. The theatre industry and its fortunes had bonded with the demands of the court and monarchy from the early 1580s, continuing under James and enhanced under Charles. When monarchy fell apart in the 1640s, so too did the idea of a coherent and distinct London theatre-land. For eighteen years from 1642 until the Restoration in 1660 there was no officially approved theatre anywhere in England. This hiatus brought an emphatic end to what had started so richly.

Besides making Shakespeare's company into the King's Men, James also made the Admiral's into Prince Henry's Men, Henry being the elder of James's two sons. Queen Anna became patron of the third adult company. The old claim that the acting companies were tolerated only in order to hone their skills ready for court performance was scotched. They could now play openly for everyone's benefit. Eventually five companies settled under Jacobean patronage, James's younger son Charles and his daughter Elizabeth getting companies in 1608 and 1610, along with the King's, Queen's and Prince Henry's Men. At first neither Charles's nor Elizabeth's companies had a theatre to play in. One moved into the old Curtain in Shoreditch, the other to the Red Bull in Clerkenwell.

17. A miniature portrait of King James I.

The Inns of Court
Plays were also popular at the Inns of Court. The training-ground for lawyers, they functioned as a third university, after Oxford and Cambridge. Two of the four Inns, Inner Temple [ML23] and Middle Temple [ML24], were located to the east of Temple Bar, while Lincoln's Inn was just north of the Strand.

18. The title page of Ben Jonson's Folio of his *Workes*. He chose to dedicate it to the Inns of Court.

Gray's Inn was on the south western edge of Gray's Inn Road. The Inns frequently invited the playing companies to perform for them for a fee. Two Shakespearean performances occurred in the Elizabethan period. The newly-formed Chamberlain's Men were requested to stage *The Comedy of Errors* in Gray's Inn at Christmas 1594, and in February 1602 *Twelfth Night* was staged at Middle Temple. Their halls offered alternative sites for early theatre. Like court performances, however, such shows were not open to the public. They entertained select audiences of trainee lawyers over their dinners. Performances at the halls are important because we can positively identify them as sites for plays. In fact, besides the outdoor and new indoor playhouses and the royal theatres at Whitehall and Hampton Court, they are the only other venues for plays in the period.

The Boys Return: A Second Wave of Child Actors
The first boy companies were stopped from playing by the beginning of the 1590s. James Burbage's new indoor playhouse at Blackfriars appeared in 1596, but was prevented by the Privy Council from showing plays using adult players. His son Richard, who inherited it, later sub-let it to two impresarios, Henry Evans and Nathaniel Giles, who wanted to start up another boy company. So the second Blackfriars opened in 1600, but with a troupe of boy players. The grandees living in Playhouse Yard found it intolerable to have adult players performing there daily, but the boys had more social cachet. A new company of St Paul's boy players had already restarted at their old playhouse in the Almoner's hall at Paul's.

For the next seven years boy companies were back in contention as players. They were more successful than the first generation of boy actors in the 1570s. Indoor venues were now more comfortable, and new playwrights were writing drama for the boys in plays like John Marston's *Antonio and Mellida*, and Thomas Middleton's *A Trick to Catch the Old One*. Soon they became notorious for satire and sexualised innuendo. Ben Jonson devised a brand of acerbic comedy different from what he wrote for the Chamberlain's Men in the 1590s. But his patience was short, and in 1606 *Volpone* was premiered at the Globe.

The boy companies at first were thought more respectable than adult players. They played less frequently, and their smaller playhouses had no reputation for crowd trouble. Although their plays could be highly erotic, the boy players were seen as relatively harmless, and their kind of entertainment allowed the normal dramatic boundaries to be extended. For a while their mockery of the court slipped under the radar.

But like the adult players the boys were at risk. Controversial plays caused a stir at court and attracted serious ire. In 1605 the Blackfriars company was reprimanded for performing *Eastward Ho!*, a collaboration by Chapman, Jonson and Marston that gave offence with its anti-Scottish comments. Over John Day's *The Isle of Gulls* in 1606 Sir Thomas Edmondes wrote that "at this time there was much speech of a play in the Blackfriars where, in the *Isle of Gulls*, from the highest to the lowest, all men's parts were acted of two divers nations." Half the boy players parodied London's courtly newcomers by adopting Scottish accents. In 1608, angered by the accumulation of political satires, James banned the boy companies both at Blackfriars and St Paul's from further playing.

A new indoor theatre opened in the Whitefriars [ML8] below Fleet Street in 1609, and the Blackfriars boys played there for several years. This short-lived venue was modelled on the earlier two indoor playhouses, but enjoyed limited success, since by 1613 we know that plays were no longer being performed there. After that the boy companies vanish from playing for ever, with a couple of exceptions in Caroline times.

The Court Masque

Theatre was not only Marlowe's and Shakespeare's plays. There was also majestic court ritual and ceremony. Royalty made 'progresses', with the court touring the country, lavishly entertained on the way at aristocratic houses. Such entertainments were a distinctive elite performance ritual throughout the period.

Once James I came to the throne the English court became centralised, mainly at Whitehall Palace. Court masques developed amazing extravagances, strongly influenced by court theatre on the continent, particularly in Italy and Spain. Masques included dances and spectacles with lavish scenery and costumes. Ben Jonson and other writers supplied the masque text (a series of speeches and choruses), while the court architect Inigo Jones supplied Italianate perspective scenery. Up to 1625 Jonson and Jones were chief writer and designer, Jones designing costumes as well as scenery for regularly devised court masques. In the Caroline period the two men fell out, Jones staying on as the mastermind behind the performance of Caroline spectacles.

19. Miniature of a Masquer.

James attended as chief observer of these events, with both of his sons dancing in the masques, while his royal consort Anna of Denmark was one of their prime movers, commissioning some and appearing in the performances herself. Since the 1970s masques have been regarded as embodying a similar force for the court to the drama of the playhouses. We should remember that impresarios like Burbage and Henslowe only flourished in London because drama became close to the hearts of the ruling courtly élite. Charles I would take this even further, the court witnessing masque performances by Queen Henrietta Maria, with for the first time the king himself participating. In this way masquing challenges our assumption that the early English stage was 'all-male'. Associating the masque

20. The Rubens Ceiling, Banqueting House, Whitehall.

with Whitehall to the west of the City is important, since many of the masques were performed at the Banqueting House [ML26], where King Charles was eventually executed. Its neo-classical design of 1622 by Inigo Jones, with its famously elaborate painted and fitted ceiling by Rubens, can still be seen today in Whitehall, a witness to the days when the Stuart dynasty used the glitter of theatrical performance to affirm its hold on power.

Ascendancy of the King's Men and Blackfriars

During the plague closure of 1608, with the boy actors expelled from Blackfriars, the King's Men were finally set to occupy their Blackfriars playhouse. James Burbage had bought the site and built the indoor theatre twelve years before, only to be banned from using it. But times had changed. By 1608 the playhouses had strong ties to the Jacobean court, so the King's Men were confident they could perform at the newly-vacated Blackfriars. Once Richard Burbage had done the necessary repairs and assigned shares in the new playhouse to his fellows who already had shares in the Globe (himself, his brother Cuthbert, John Heminges, William Shakespeare and Henry Condell), after a long plague epidemic ended the actors started putting on plays there in late 1609, or early 1610.

For the first time a company had not one but two play-houses, one of which allowed adult actors to perform in the refined atmosphere of an indoor, candle-lit playhouse with its increased sense of élitism. At Blackfriars the heightened cost of admission meant that they now performed for the top end of London's audiences. Their new venue was associated in the public mind with richer playgoers and sophisticated music before and during performances.

By returning to their 1595 plan of having two playhouses, one indoor, one outdoor, the King's Men could now look toward a significant growth in their income. The Blackfriars was close to the wealthy law students at the Inns of Court, and to James's court at Whitehall. They could afford to use one playhouse while the other was closed, alternating their playing between the Globe in the summer months and the Blackfriars in the win-ter. This was a luxury no other playing company could afford.

While the boy actors played at Blackfriars it acquired a good reputation for music and song. The distinguished Blackfriars theatre musicians acquired music from composers like Martin Peerson, Richard Johnson and John Milton (senior). The King's Men kept on the Blackfriars music ensemble that they inher-ited from the boy company. The Globe's stage balcony then gained a music room to match the Blackfriars.

21. Portrait of John Fletcher, who succeeded William Shakespeare as the King's Men's leading dramatist when Shakespeare retired in 1613–14. By an unknown artist, *c.*1620.

Jacobean 'Citizen Playhouses'

The other outdoor theatres, particularly the Fortune, Red Bull and the older Curtain, all to the north of the City, by now had gained a distinct reputation. Theatre historians have characterised them as 'citizen playhouses' catering for the lower orders of the London community. Such audiences preferred the old plays. The Fortune continued to stage the classics by Kyd and Marlowe. Working men and women enjoyed *The Spanish Tragedy* or *Tamburlaine* at the Fortune, just as the previous generation had done in the late 1580s at the Rose on Bankside. In 1620 it was said that "men go to the Fortune in Golding Lane to see the Tragedy of Doctor Faustus. There indeed a man may behold shag-haired devils run roaring over the stage with squibs in their mouths, while drummers make thunder in the tiring house and the twelve penny hirelings made artificial lightning in their heavens."

Other playwrights at the Red Bull provided texts for a similar citizen audience as the Fortune, though that should not diminish the artistry and passion of such Jacobean plays. All plays are written for an audience, not in the abstract. A number of Red Bull plays were authored by the talented Thomas Heywood, a theatre poet whose two parts of *If You Know Not Me, You Know Nobody* (1604–5) had an admiring reception.

Such performances maximized nostalgia for the former greatness of Elizabeth's time, coinciding as it did with the Jacobean court's mire, rocked by scandals sometimes of a sexual nature. Heywood's *A Woman Killed With Kindness* from about 1603 gave an onstage voice to the less privileged in society, staging an adulterous relationship and its aftermath in a domestic rather than a courtly setting.

22. The title page of Middleton and Dekker's *The Roaring Girl*, showing Moll Frith.

As the 1600s moved into its second decade, John Dekker and Thomas Middleton wrote for the Fortune a collaborative effort called *The Roaring Girl*, a play creating uproar by dramatizing the real-life actions of one Marion Frith (popularly known as 'Moll Cutpurse'). The play, performed by Prince Henry's Men, made the most of Frith's reputation as a thief dressed in male clothing, a fact that the title-page highlighted when the play appeared in print in 1611. At one performance of the play Frith went on the stage "in man's apparel and played upon her lute and sang a song", making her the first woman to appear on a public stage.

John Webster's *The White Devil* (1611) was poorly received at the Red Bull. In its printed edition Webster made it clear he felt the playhouse had been the wrong place for his darkly sophisticated revenge tragedy. In the following year his *The Duchess of Malfi* was launched by the King's Men at the more exclusive Blackfriars.

Later Jacobean Stability, and the Hope
After the Blackfriars opened for the King's Men in 1609/10 came a time of stability. It began to feel like a consolidating, mature theatrical industry. In 1614 Edward Alleyn and Philip Henslowe decided to build the Hope on Bankside [ML21]. This was the first (and last) dual-purpose theatre; replacing an old bear-

23. Shakespeare, the engraving in the 1623 Folio of his plays, drawn by Martin Droeshout.

baiting house, and designed for both baiting and plays. The contract to build the Hope was signed within a month of the adjacent Globe burning down. Designed with a removable stage for bear-baiting as well as plays, the Hope soon encountered problems from the animals and their accompanying smells. Eventually it stopped plays, remaining only for bear-baiting. One striking image we have of the problems at the Hope, thanks to its dual-purpose design, comes from the printed edition of Ben Jonson's *Bartholomew Fair*, performed there by the Lady Elizabeth's Men. Jonson made it clear he was not happy with the new venue as a setting for plays and playing.

The short-lived Hope was the last of the outdoor theatres. The success of the King's Men at the indoor Blackfriars now showed the way forward. The later Cockpit [ML9] and Salisbury Court indoor theatres [ML10] both copied its design.

The Rise of Indoor Values

In 1616, the year of Shakespeare's death, one of his former literary rivals published a grand book of his own plays and poetry. Ben Jonson called this Folio edition his *Works*, meaning that for the first time a poet and playwright was exhibiting his whole literary output. Unlike quartos, folios were large and expensive

24. The list of 35 Shakespeare plays printed in the first Folio of 1623.

A CATALOGVE

of the feuerall Comedies, Histories, and Tragedies contained in this Volume.

COMEDIES.		The First part of King Henry the fourth.	46
		The Second part of K. Henry the fourth.	74
The Tempest.	Folio 1.	The Life of King Henry the Fift.	69
The two Gentlemen of Verona.	20	The First part of King Henry the Sixt.	96
The Merry Wiues of Windsor.	38	The Second part of King Hen. the Sixt.	120
Measure for Measure.	61	The Third part of King Henry the Sixt.	147
The Comedy of Errours.	85	The Life & Death of Richard the Third.	173
Much adoo about Nothing.	101	The Life of King Henry the Eight.	205
Loues Labour lost.	122	TRAGEDIES.	
Midsommer Nights Dreame.	145		
The Merchant of Venice.	163	The Tragedy of Coriolanus.	Fol. 1.
As you Like it.	185	Titus Andronicus.	31
The Taming of the Shrew.	208	Romeo and Juliet.	53
All is well, that Ends well.	230	Timon of Athens.	80
Twelfe-Night, or what you will.	255	The Life and death of Julius Cæsar.	109
The Winters Tale.	304	The Tragedy of Macbeth.	131
		The Tragedy of Hamlet.	152
HISTORIES.		King Lear.	283
		Othello, the Moore of Venice.	310
The Life and Death of King John.	Fol. 1.	Anthony and Cleopater.	346
The Life & death of Richard the second.	23	Cymbeline King of Britaine.	369

books to purchase. A quarto cost only sixpence, whereas a folio cost as much as a pound. So influential was Jonson's publication that seven years later in 1623 two members of the King's Men, Shakespeare's ex-colleagues John Heminges and Henry Condell produced a Folio of Shakespeare's plays, 'Mr. William Shakespeares Comedies, Histories, & Tragedies.' Without this compilation, half of Shakespeare's forty plays would have been lost forever.

Although the playhouses were advancing economically and socially, we should not forget the lower social range they now catered to. By 1617 Red Bull proprietor Christopher Beeston emulated the King's Men at Blackfriars by building an indoor theatre in Drury Lane (the first in the West End of London) aimed at the well-to-do playgoing audience [ML9]. On the Shrove Tuesday holiday of 1617 a gang of apprentices, objecting to Beeston's transfer of the Red Bull plays to the pricy new Cockpit, attacked it, burning and half demolishing it before City officials intervened. One of the apprentices was shot dead. Beeston soon reopened the Cockpit (also known as the Phoenix because it was reborn from the flames), and it flourished as the only serious rival to the Blackfriars. This clash of financial ambition and audience allegiance shows the changing nature of London theatre. The entertainment industry was now firmly part of the capital's existence.

We must add one more incident of London's theatre. It created a stage sensation and an outrage for the authorities. In 1624, Thomas Middleton's *A Game at Chess* played at the Globe to huge audiences for a unique run of nine days in a row. It was a stunning sellout. Gary Taylor has estimated that its run may have been attended by one-seventh of London's whole population.

The eagerness with which Londoners flocked to see the play came from King James's attempt to negotiate a marriage between the Prince of Wales and the Infanta of Spain. Middleton represented this in his play as a Spanish plot to undermine England's Protestant state. Deeply unpopular with London's anti-Spanish crowds, the eventual failure of the marriage plan induced displays of public celebration. Middleton's mockery included the former Spanish ambassador, and when his successor complained to James, the play was stopped. Middleton himself escaped being put in prison for it, but his son was arrested instead. Quarto copies of the play survive, one with an autograph note telling the story of the "nyne dayse" when it is claimed the Globe took "fiveteene hundred pounde". This is probably an exaggeration, but the story shows how plays could arouse public emotions, not to mention the financial gains when a show chimes with the popular mood.

25. The title page of *A Game at Chess* by Thomas Middleton, showing the figures as they appeared on stage.

The Caroline Stage:
The Final Act of the Shakespearean Theatres

26. Portrait of King Charles and Henrietta Maria.

THE 'CAROLINE' PERIOD covers the years 1625 to 1642, when Charles Stuart, son of James I, was king. Although he reigned on through the civil war until his public execution in 1649, 1642 is the endpoint for our story of the Shakespearean London theatres, because with the outbreak of war in that year Parliament closed all of the Shakespearean playhouses and banned playing. With the 1660 Restoration of Charles II, Charles's eldest son, a different kind of theatre arrived.

From 1625, when Charles assumed the throne upon his father's decease, James's only surviving son continued royal patronage for the theatre. A massive epidemic of the plague had coincided with the old king's death – John Fletcher the playwright is thought to have been one of its victims – so most acting companies had to restart completely. Only the King's Men renewed their elite status under Charles.

The Birth of Caroline Theatre

The new companies did well too, though only one new theatre appeared when the Salisbury Court [ML10] was opened in 1629 by Richard Gunnell and William Blagrave. The three indoor theatres – Blackfriars, Cockpit, Salisbury Court – were distinct, socially and in their richer clientele, from the Globe on Bankside and the two open-air northern theatres, the Red Bull and the Fortune. Much cheaper, the outdoor venues became part of a related but distinct theatrical scene for the lower classes. A new wave of Caroline writers appeared, including William Davenant, Richard Brome, Philip Massinger, and James Shirley. The title pages of many plays in print now proclaimed performance at indoor rather than outdoor theatres. Whereas some still announced performances at the Globe, very few mention performances at the Red Bull or the Fortune.

Massinger, John Ford, and Ben Jonson returned to the public stage, and Jonson's former assistant Richard Brome wrote for the indoor theatres, while at the outdoor theatres the long-established classics were being restaged, including the old hits by Marlowe and Kyd. At the Blackfriars, Shakespeare became rather less popular than Fletcher and the newcomer William Davenant.

A Cavalier Theatre?

Throughout this period the King's Men continued exactly as they had under James, enjoying their unique resource of owning and performing in both indoor and outdoor theatres. They benefited from having the country's leading patron. The four visits of Charles's consort Queen Henrietta Maria to the Blackfriars characterizes the rise of elite female spectators and the growth of styles of play aimed at female tastes.

Easily the busiest and most self-advertizing of the new talents was William Davenant. Claiming to be an illegitimate son of Shakespeare (his beautiful mother was hostess of a tavern in Oxford where it was said the Bard used to stay while en route to Stratford), Davenant was certainly a loyal supporter of the king, writing masques as well as plays to suit his taste. Philip Massinger was the main alternative. As a Jacobean writer, Massinger collaborated with Fletcher and others, and after 1625 succeeded Fletcher as the King's Men's chief playwright. Massinger advertized the perils of acting in his first Caroline play, *The Roman Actor* (1626) at Blackfriars.

27. Miniature of
Henrietta Maria.

Richard Brome also wrote Blackfriars plays in the late 1620s. But from 1630 to 1637 Davenant made himself the main producer of their new plays. He exemplifies the rise of elitism in 1630s theatre. His plays were full of fashionable wit and charm, especially his 1633 comedy, *The Wits*.

At the Blackfriars in Caroline times the King's Men provided an artistic cocktail of aesthetics and delight, deploying music and spectacle as well as their repertory of great plays. They employed their own consort of musicians, said to be the best in town. The famous lawyer Bulstrode Whitelocke, writing in the 1630s, had this to report on the Blackfriars and its use of music. He declared:

> I was so conversant with the musicians, and so willing to gain their favour, especially at this time, that I composed an air myself, with the assistance of Mr Ives [the famous composer], and called it *Whitelock's Coranto*, which being cried up, was first played publicly by the Blackfri-

ars Music, who were then esteemed the best of the common musicians in London. Whenever I came to that house (as I did sometimes in those days), though not often, to see a play, the musicians would presently play *Whitelock's Coranto*, and it was so often called for that they would have played it twice or thrice in an afternoon.

This says something about the social and cultural value of frequenting the Blackfriars.

Beeston's Theatres: the Cockpit

The other companies also ran healthily through this last period. Christopher Beeston, a player in the early Shakespeare company up to 1600, from 1612 had led Queen Anna's Men at the Red Bull. In 1616 he set up an indoor theatre, a copy of Blackfriars, in Drury Lane. He managed both the outdoor Red Bull and indoor Cockpit. But through the later Jacobean period and the Caroline years the two Beeston theatres gained very different reputations. The elite Cockpit attracted a different society from what was now being called a citizen playhouse, the Red Bull. Yet the two theatres shared plays, players and playwrights throughout the reign of King Charles. Only the audiences differed.

In 1626 the Cockpit/Phoenix reopened with a new playing company, Queen Henrietta's Men, named after Charles's new queen. In August 1628 the king's favourite, the Duke of Buckingham, went there to see Heywood's *The Rape of Lucrece*. As Charles's right-hand man in 1624 he had accompanied the prince on their foolish and secret journey to Madrid to meet Charles's promised wife, the Infanta of Spain. After the king, Buckingham was the most powerful man in England (later that year he was assassinated by an aggrieved army officer). Buckingham's visit established the Cockpit / Phoenix as one of the leading social venues.

Although Beeston's indoor theatre did well in competition with its glamorous rival the Blackfriars, the Caroline playing companies often moved between indoor and outdoor venues. Red Bull plays were printed with a fictionally heightened status as Cockpit/Phoenix plays. A new boy company, the Children of the Revels, played at the Salisbury Court (third of the indoor venues), and another boy company arrived in the later Caroline era, when Beeston, presumably thinking that boys would be easier to manage than adult players, ejected his adult company and in their place installed the so-called 'Beeston's Boys' at the Cockpit. In reality this company also featured six adults. Throughout this time the Fortune went on staging *Tamburlaine* and *The Spanish Tragedy*, while the Red Bull also continued with the older over-the-top drama. Their survival all the way to the closure indicates that outdoor theatre maintained its impact on theatrical culture until the very end of the Shakespearean playhouses.

The Salisbury Court Playhouse

A third indoor playhouse, the Salisbury Court, opened in 1629 not far from the Blackfriars. At different times it was home to a company of youngsters, the Children of the Revels, and to various adult companies, including in the later 1630s Queen Henrietta Maria's Men. Owned by Richard Gunnell the ex-Fortune player, and William Blagrave, Yeoman of the Revels, it profited from the now-lucrative market of indoor theatre. Although its reputation was less than that of the Blackfriars and Cockpit, several notable playwrights worked there, including Richard Brome, who in 1635 was contracted to deliver three plays a year to Henrietta Maria's company, including his *Antipodes* of 1638.

Staging Witchcraft at the Caroline Theatres

All of the London theatres were keen to exploit anxiety and wonder on a broad spread of contemporary issues. Jacobean plays, like Shakespeare's *Macbeth* and one by the collaborative team of Rowley, Dekker and Ford, *The Witch of Edmonton*, had been able to make capital out of the current fascination with witchcraft. So too did Caroline writers. In August 1634 the King's Men staged at the Globe a play by Heywood and Brome about the recent witch trials in Lancashire. *The Witches of Lancashire* is known to have played for three successive days, suggesting great popularity. The story of the alleged witches was a sensation, and the King's Men persuaded the Master of the Revels to ban a rival company's play until their own had had its month on the stage first.

This comic tale of magical trickery staged the story of four contemporary women who had recently been brought to London for re-trial from Pendle Forest in Lancashire (they had been found guilty of witchcraft, but Archbishop Laud and others doubted the charge). The two King's Men's authors were somehow given access to the witness statements and the accused's defences. The play succeeded partly because

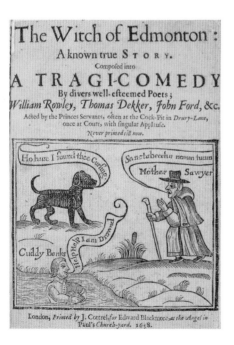

28. Title page of Rowley, Dekker and Ford's *The Witch of Edmonton*, 1658.

of its hot-off-the-press narrative. This and the rival play on the same subject were both printed later that year. Theatre provided what its consumerist audience, both as spectators and readers, wanted.

Caroline Court Theatre: Renaissance Aesthetics, Whitehall Masquing Culture and the New Cockpit-in-Court

Under Charles and Henrietta Maria, court theatre flourished even more richly than it had under James. Both of the new rulers were keen on theatre and display, especially Henrietta Maria, who had been raised at court in France, with its lavish tastes. Masques symbolized the ideology and power of the Stuart courts.

Charles's court extended the expense and splendour of the masque beyond even the spectacles of the Jacobean court. Charles saw himself as the prime political authority in England and Scotland, which would cause him great harm in the later 1640s. He wanted to present his glory as an idealized monarch in the European tradition. He set about amassing one of the largest and finest art collections in Europe, including great portraiture, the famous Rubens ceiling in the Banqueting House at Whitehall, and many fine statues and tapestries. He hired one of the greatest painters in Europe, Anthony van Dyck, to be his principal court artist, who subsequently produced some images of the Caroline court and its leading aristocrats. The visual splendour and flashiness of the Caroline court masque manifested the kind of European court Charles wished to foreground.

29. View of Whitehall from St James's Park by Hendrick Danckerts, showing to the right the six-sided Cockpit-in-Court theatre with lantern-style roof.

The public stage renewed its link with the activities of the court in 1629, when Inigo Jones was instructed to rebuild the old Cockpit-in-Court [ML27] in Whitehall Palace. It opened for plays in November 1630. It was designed for the leading companies to perform narrative tales to an exclusive courtly audience. It had a royal dais with private access down a special stairway, so that the king could sit together with Henrietta Maria facing the stage, his courtiers and ambassadors all round him. The Cockpit-in-Court staged numerous dramatic works for the king, including some of the classics by Marlowe, Heywood, Fletcher, Jonson, Ford, Beaumont and Fletcher, Webster, Massinger and Dekker.

30. C. Walter Hodges's drawing of the Cockpit-in-Court.

Closure, War and Restoration

In September 1642 Parliament stopped all playing, announcing that such frivolities were wrong in such a fraught political time. For the next eighteen years the playhouses remained closed, until the monarchy was restored in 1660, although plays and other entertainments were sometimes staged covertly at the Red Bull and other playhouses. Staging plays became seen as a wilful act of political subversion. In 1649 the defeated Charles was beheaded on a platform stage outside his own Banqueting House, a grisly event that again linked theatre and spectacle to monarchy. England now became a republic without a king. Oliver Cromwell was soon to serve as Lord Protector, followed after his death by his son Richard, who failed to sustain the republic successfully.

Monarchy was restored in 1660 when Charles II assumed the throne. The king's return to London meant that he brought back theatre immediately. It was seen as a return to normality. William Davenant, restored along with the king to London's theatre-land, was one of the two impresarios the king designated to develop the new theatre. He had already tried to set up a new variety of play in 1658 and 1659, full of dance and song, its best exemplar being *The Siege of Rhodes*. Since the word 'play' was still viewed with hostility, he called his new work 'opera'. He and his opposite, Thomas Killigrew, mounted more musical versions of plays, including those of Shakespeare.

31. Sir William Davenant, playwright and impresario, with his famous syphilitic nose.

With the outdoor theatres all gone, Restoration drama followed the trend set by the indoor Shakespearean playhouses. Audiences became more exclusive. Different ways of thinking about theatre accompanied the returned royalist exiles from Paris in 1660. The Restoration stage abandoned the Shakespearean model of an audience surrounding the actors on all sides. The old plays were restaged, but rewritten for the new theatres. New actors and writers began to run a fresh type of scenic theatre. It centred itself in the West End and Drury Lane, which survives today as London's modern theatre-land.

32. Title page of *Eikon Basilici*, 1649.

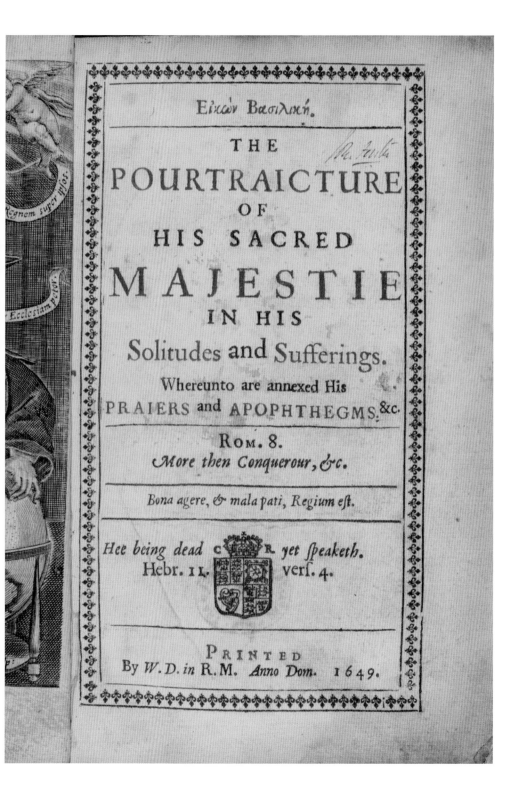

Εἰκὼν Βασιλική.

THE
POURTRAICTURE
OF
HIS SACRED
MAJESTIE
IN HIS

Solitudes and Sufferings.

Whereunto are annexed His
PRAIERS and APOPHTHEGMS, &c.

ROM. 8.
More then Conquerour, &c.

Bona agere, & mala pati, Regium est.

Hee being dead C R yet speaketh.
Hebr. 1 I. verf. 4.

PRINTED
By *W. D. in R. M.* Anno Dom. 1649.

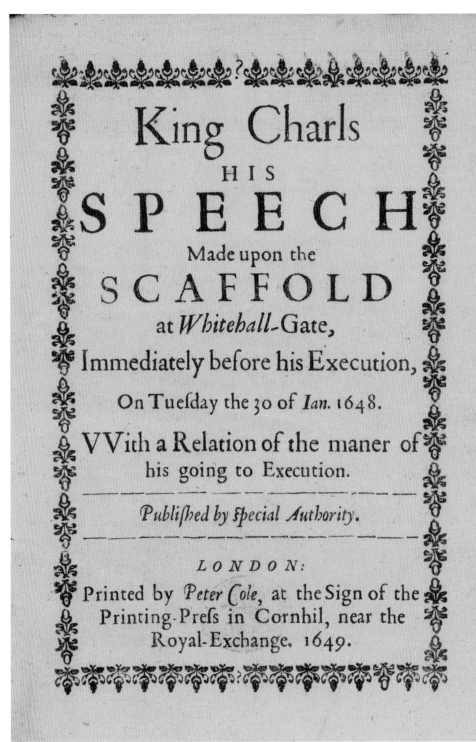

King Charls

HIS

SPEECH

Made upon the

SCAFFOLD

at *Whitehall*-Gate,

Immediately before his Execution,

On Tuesday the 30 of *Ian.* 1648.

VVith a Relation of the maner of
his going to Execution.

Published by special Authority.

LONDON:

Printed by *Peter Cole*, at the Sign of the
Printing-Press in Cornhil, near the
Royal-Exchange. 1649.

Further Reading and Information:

John Astington, *Actors and Acting in Shakespeare's time:
the art of stage playing.* Cambridge University Press, 2010.

Julian Bowsher and Pat Miller, *The Rose and the Globe –
playhouses of Shakespeare's Bankside, Southwark.*
Museum of London Archaeology, 2009.

Julian Bowsher, *Shakespeare's London Theatreland.*
Museum of London Archaeology, 2012.

Andrew Gurr, *Playgoing in Shakespeare's London.*
Cambridge University Press, third edition, 2004.

Andrew Gurr, *The Shakespearean Stage 1594-1642.*
Cambridge University Press, fourth edition, 2009.

The Oxford Handbook of Early Modern Theatre, ed. Richard
Dutton. Oxford University Press, 2009.

Peter Womack, *English Renaissance Drama.*
Blackwell Publishing, 2006

Websites

http://shalt.org.uk/
Shakespearean London Theatres (ShaLT) AHRC funded
project.

http://www.henslowe-alleyn.org.uk/index.html
The Henslowe-Alleyn Digitisation Project.

http://www.ortelia.com/RoseTheatre.htm
3D interactive models of the Rose theatre designed for early
modern drama research projects at University of Queensland,
Australia.

http://www.ortelia.com/BoarsHead.html
3D interactive models of the Boar's Head theatre designed for
early modern drama research projects at University of
Queensland, Australia.

33. Title page of
*King Charles his
Speech Made Upon
the Scaffold*, 1649.

Acknowledgements

This edition first published by
Shakespearean London Theatres (ShaLT) in 2013
De Montfort University, The Gateway, Leicester, LE1 9BH
http://shalt.org.uk

ISBN: 978 0 9575379 0 3

Project management by Dr Maurice Hindle
Designed by Nigel Soper
Production management by Geoff Barlow
Printed in the UK

10 9 8 7 6 5 4 3 2 1

We should like to thank the following for their kind permission to reproduce
the illustrations:
Title page © Yale Center for British Art, Paul Mellon Collection,
New Haven, Connecticut.
Plate 1 © The Syndics of The Fitzwilliam Museum, Cambridge.
Plates 2, 4, 5, 8, 10, 11, 13, 15, 16, 17, 18, 19, 22, 23, 24, 25, 26, 27, 28, 31,
32, 33 © The Trustees of the Victoria and Albert Museum, London.
Plates 3, 6, 30 © The Folger Shakespeare Library, Washington.
Front cover and Plate 7 © William Dudley (a reconstructive cutaway
view of the first Rose incorporating material by John Greenfield and
C. Walter Hodges).
Plate 9 © The Master and Fellows of Corpus Christi College, Cambridge,
who cannot vouch for the identity of the portrait.
Plate 12 © Guildhall Library, City of London.
Plates 14, 21 © National Portrait Gallery, London.
Plate 20 © The Banqueting House and Historic Royal Palaces.
Plate 29 © UK Government Art Collection, Department for Culture,
Media and Sport.
Inside front cover and Inside back cover flap © The National Library of
Sweden, Maps and Pictures DeLaG89

Front cover. A cutaway illustration,
showing what the Rose playhouse o
Bankside might have looked like in i
original form before 1592.

Front cover flap. A detail of a stain
glass window in St. Giles Church,
Cripplegate, depicting how the
Fortune playhouse may have looked

Inside front cover. A detail from an
engraving by John Norden dated
1600, showing the area around St
Mary Overie, Southwark, and the
London Bridge.

Back cover. Title page for *The
Merchant of Venice*, first published
in quarto in 1600. The description o
its story probably resembles the
playbills posted to advertise it.

Inside back cover flap. A detail fro
the Norden engraving on the inside
front cover giving a street view of t
City of London.

Frontispiece. A portrait, thought b
some to be of Christopher Marlowe
discovered thirty years ago behind
fireplace in Corpus Christi College
Cambridge, where Marlowe was a
student.

Title page. A sketch drawing by
Wenceslas Hollar of Bankside,
Southwark (*c.*1638), in preparation f
his 1647 'Long View' engraving of
London.

Page 4. Portrait of John Fletcher, w
succeeded William Shakespeare as
the King's Men's leading dramatist
when Shakespeare retired in 1613–1
By an unknown artist, *c.*1620.

Shakespearean London Theatres is an AHRC funded project in association with De Montfort
University Leicester and the V&A Museum's Theatre & Performance Department.